The Sacraments

A Ch

GW00703508

Pope Francis

All booklets are published thanks to the generous support of the members of the Catholic Truth Society

CATHOLIC TRUTH SOCIETY

PUBLISHERS TO THE HOLY SEE

Contents

Baptism and Christian Initiation 3

Baptism Continued 7

Confirmation 11

The Eucharist 15

How to experience the Eucharist 18

The Sacrament of Reconciliation 22

The Sacrament of the Anointing of the Sick 27

Holy Orders 31

Matrimony 35

ISBN 978 1 78469 000 7

Baptism and Christian Initiation

Baptism is the Sacrament on which our very faith is founded and which grafts us as a living member onto Christ and his Church. Together with the Eucharist and Confirmation it forms what is known as "Christian initiation", like one great sacramental event that configures us to the Lord and turns us into a living sign of his presence and of his love.

Is Baptism necessary?

Yet a question may stir within us: is Baptism really necessary to live as Christians and follow Jesus? After all, isn't it merely a ritual, a formal act of the Church in order to give a name to the little boy or girl? This question can arise. And on this point what the Apostle Paul writes is illuminating: "Do you not know that all of us who have been baptised into Christ Jesus were baptised into his death? We were buried therefore with him by baptism into death, so that as Christ was raised from the dead by the glory of the Father, we too might walk in newness of life" (*Rm* 6:3-4). Therefore, it is not a formality! It is an act that touches the depths of our existence. A baptised child and an unbaptised child are not the same. A person who is baptised and a person who is not baptised are not the same.

We, by Baptism, are immersed in that inexhaustible source of life which is the death of Jesus, the greatest act of love in all of history; and thanks to this love we can live a new life, no longer at the mercy of evil, of sin and of death, but in communion with God and with our brothers and sisters.

We should remember our Baptism

Many of us have no memory of the celebration of this Sacrament, and it is obvious why, if we were baptised soon after birth. I have asked this question two or three times already, here, in this square: who among you knows the date of your Baptism, raise your hands. It is important to know the day on which I was immersed in that current of Jesus's salvation. And I will allow myself to give you some advice... but, more than advice, a task for today. Today, at home, go look, ask about the date of your Baptism and that way you will keep in mind that most beautiful day of Baptism. To know the date of our Baptism is to know a blessed day. The danger of not knowing is that we can lose awareness of what the Lord has done in us, the memory of the gift we have received. Thus, we end up considering it only as an event that took place in the past - and not by our own will but by that of our parents - and that it has no impact on the present. We must reawaken the memory of our Baptism. We are called to live out our Baptism every day as the present reality of our lives. If we manage to follow Jesus and to remain in the Church, despite our limitations and with our weaknesses and our sins, it is precisely in the Sacrament whereby we have become new creatures and have been clothed in Christ. It is by the power of Baptism, in fact, that, freed of original sin, we are inserted into Jesus's relation to God the Father; that we are bearers of a new hope, for Baptism gives us this new hope: the hope of going on the path of salvation our whole life long. And this hope nothing and no one can extinguish, for it is a hope that does not disappoint. Remember, hope in the Lord never disappoints. Thanks to Baptism, we are capable of forgiving and of loving even those who offend us and do evil to us. By our Baptism, we recognise in the least and in the poor the face of the Lord who visits us and makes himself close. Baptism helps us to recognise in the face of the needy, the suffering, and also of our neighbour, the face of Jesus. All this is possible thanks to the power of Baptism!

Can I baptise myself?

A last point, which is important. I ask you a question: can a person baptise him or herself? No one can be self-baptised! No one. We can ask for it, desire it, but we always need someone else to confer this Sacrament in the name of the Lord. For Baptism is a gift which is bestowed in a context of care and fraternal sharing. Throughout history, one baptises another, another and another... it is a chain. A chain of Grace. I cannot baptise myself: I must ask another for Baptism. It is an act of brotherhood, an act of filiation to the Church. In the celebration of Baptism we can see the most genuine features of the Church, who like a mother continues to give birth to new children in Christ, in the fecundity of the Holy Spirit.

Let us, then, ask the Lord from our hearts that we may be able to experience ever more, in everyday life, this grace that we have received at Baptism. That in encountering us, our brothers and sisters may encounter true children of God, true brothers and sisters of Jesus Christ, true members of the Church. And do not forget your homework today: find out, ask for the date of your Baptism. As I know my birthday, I should know my Baptism day, because it is a feast day.

Baptism Continued

I would like pause again on Baptism, in order to stress an important fruit of this Sacrament: it makes us members of the Body of Christ and of the People of God. St Thomas Aquinas states that whoever receives Baptism is incorporated in Christ, almost as one of his own limbs, and becomes aggregated to the community of the faithful (cf. *Summa Theologiae*, III, q. 69, art. 5; q. 70, art. 1), that is, the People of God. In the school of the Second Vatican Council, we say today that Baptism allows us *to enter the People of God*, to become members of a People on a journey, a *people on pilgrimage* through history.

Baptism passes faith to our children

In effect, as from generation to generation life is transmitted, so too from generation to generation, through rebirth at the baptismal font, grace is transmitted, and by this grace the Christian People journeys through time, like a river that irrigates the land and spreads God's blessing throughout the world. From the moment that Jesus said what we heard in the Gospel Reading, the disciples went out to baptise; and from that time until today there is a chain in the transmission of the faith through Baptism.

And each one of us is a link in that chain: a step forward, always; like a river that irrigates. Such is the grace of God and such is our faith, which we must transmit to our sons and daughters, transmit to children, so that once adults, they can do the same for their children. This is what Baptism is. Why? Because Baptism lets us enter this People of God that transmits the faith. This is very important. A People of God that journeys and hands down the faith.

Baptism and mission

In virtue of Baptism we become *missionary disciples*, called to bring the Gospel to the world (cf. Apostolic Exhortation *Evangelii Gaudium*, n. 120). "All the baptised, whatever their position in the Church or their level of instruction in the faith, are agents of evangelisation.... The new evangelisation calls for personal involvement" (*ibid.*) from everyone, the whole of the People of God, a new kind of personal involvement on the part of each of the baptised. The People of God is *a disciple People* - because it receives the faith - and *a missionary People* - because it transmits the faith. And this is what Baptism works in us: it gives us Grace and hands on the faith to us. All of us in the Church are disciples, and this we are forever, our whole lifelong; and we are all missionaries, each in the place the Lord has assigned to him or her. Everyone: the littlest one is also a missionary; and the one who seems to be the greatest is a disciple.

But one of you might say: "Bishops are not disciples, Bishops know everything; the Pope knows everything, he is not a disciple". No, the Bishops and the Pope must also be disciples, because if they are not disciples, they do no good. They cannot be missionaries, they cannot transmit the faith. We must all be disciples and missionaries.

There exists an indissoluble bond between the *mystical* and the *missionary* dimension of the Christian vocation, both rooted in Baptism. "Upon receiving faith and Baptism, we Christians accept the action of the Holy Spirit who leads to confessing Jesus as Son of God and calling God 'Abba', Father.... All of us who are baptised ... are called to live and transmit communion with the Trinity, for evangelisation is a calling to participate in the communion of the Trinity" (*Final Document of Aparecida*, n. 157).

Baptism and Community

No one is saved by himself. We are the community of believers, we are the People of God and in this community we share the beauty of the experience of a love that precedes us all, but that at the same time calls us to be "channels" of grace for one another, despite our limitations and our sins. The communitarian dimension is not just a "frame", an "outline", but an integral part of Christian life, of witness and of evangelisation. The Christian faith is born and lives in the Church, and in Baptism families and parishes celebrate the incorporation of a new member in Christ and in his Body which is the Church (cf. *ibid.*, n. 175b).

On the subject of the importance of Baptism for the People of God, the history of the *Christian community in Japan* is exemplary. It suffered severe persecution at the start of the 17th century. There were many martyrs, members of the clergy were expelled and thousands of faithful killed. No priest was left in Japan, they were all expelled. Then the community retreated into hiding, keeping the faith and prayer in seclusion. And when a child was born, the father or mother baptised him or her, because the faithful can baptise in certain circumstances. When, after roughly two and a half centuries, 250 years later, missionaries returned to Japan, thousands of Christians stepped out into the open and the Church was able to flourish again. They survived by the grace of Baptism! This is profound: the People of God transmits the faith, baptises her children and goes forward. And they maintained, even in secret, a strong communal spirit, because their Baptism had made of them one single body in Christ: they were isolated and hidden, but they were always members of the People of God, members of the Church. Let us learn a great deal from this history!

Confirmation

In this third catechesis on the Sacraments, we pause to reflect on Confirmation or "Chrismation", which must be understood in continuity with Baptism, to which it is inseparably linked. These two Sacraments, together with the Eucharist, form a single saving event - called "Christian initiation" - in which we are inserted into Jesus Christ, who died and rose, and become new creatures and members of the Church. This is why these three Sacraments were originally celebrated on one occasion, at the end of the catechumenal journey, normally at the Easter Vigil. The path of formation and gradual insertion into the Christian community, which could last even up to a few years, was thus sealed. One travelled step by step to reach Baptism, then Confirmation and the Eucharist.

Anointed like Christ

We commonly speak of the sacrament of "Chrismation", a word that signifies "anointing". And, in effect, through the oil called "sacred Chrism" we are conformed, in the power of the Spirit, to Jesus Christ, who is the only true "anointed One", the "Messiah", the Holy One of God. The word "Confirmation" then reminds us that this Sacrament brings an increase and deepening of baptismal grace: it unites us more firmly to Christ, it renders our bond with the Church more perfect, and it gives us a special strength of the Holy Spirit to spread and defend the faith, ... to confess the name of Christ boldly, and never to be ashamed of his Cross (cf. *Catechism of the Catholic Church*, n. 1303).

For this reason, it is important to take care that our children, our young people, receive this sacrament. We all take care that they are baptised and this is good, but perhaps we do not take so much care to ensure that they are confirmed. Thus they remain at a midpoint in their journey and do not receive the Holy Spirit, who is so important in the Christian life since he gives us the strength to go on. Let us think a little, each one of us: do we truly care whether our children, our young people, receive Confirmation? This is important, it is important! And if you have children or adolescents at home who have not yet received it and are at the age to do so, do everything possible to ensure that they complete their Christian initiation and receive the power of the Holy Spirit. It is important!

Preparing to welcome the Holy Spirit

Naturally it is important to prepare those being confirmed well, leading them towards a personal commitment to faith in Christ and reawakening in them a sense of belonging to the Church.

Confirmation, like every Sacrament, is not the work

of men but of God, who cares for our lives in such a manner as to mould us in the image of his Son, to make us capable of loving like him. He does it by infusing his in us his Holy Spirit, whose action pervades the whole person and his entire life, as reflected in the seven gifts that Tradition, in light of the Sacred Scripture, has always highlighted. These seven gifts: I do not want to ask you if you remember the seven gifts. Perhaps you will all know them... But I will say them on your behalf. What are these gifts? Wisdom, Understanding, Counsel, Fortitude, Knowledge, Piety and Fear of the Lord. And these gifts have been given to us precisely with the Holy Spirit in the Sacrament of Confirmation. I therefore intend to dedicate the catecheses that follow those on the Sacrament to these seven gifts.

Christ acts through us

When we welcome the Holy Spirit into our hearts and allow him to act, Christ makes himself present in us and takes shape in our lives; through us, it will be he - Christ himself - who prays, forgives, gives hope and consolation, serves the brethren, draws close to the needy and to the least, creates community and sows peace. Think how important this is: by means of the Holy Spirit, Christ himself comes to do all this among us and for us. That is why it is important that children and young people receive the Sacrament of Confirmation.

Dear brothers and sisters, let us remember that we have received Confirmation! All of us! Let us remember it, first in order to thank the Lord for this gift, and then to ask him to help us to live as true Christians, to walk always with joy in the Holy Spirit who has been given to us.

The Eucharist

The Eucharist is at the heart of "Christian initiation", together with Baptism and Confirmation, and it constitutes the source of the Church's life itself. From this Sacrament of love, in fact, flows every authentic journey of faith, of communion and of witness.

A feast of Word and Bread

What we see when we gather to celebrate the Eucharist, the Mass, already gives us an intuition of what we are about to live. At the centre of the space intended for the celebration there is an altar, which is a table covered with a tablecloth, and this makes us think of a banquet. On the table there is a cross to indicate that on this altar what is offered is the sacrifice of Christ: he is the spiritual food that we receive there, under the species of bread and wine. Beside the table is the ambo, the place from which the Word of God is proclaimed: and this indicates that there we gather to listen to the Lord who speaks through Sacred Scripture, and therefore the food that we receive is also his Word.

Word and Bread in the Mass become one, as at the Last Supper, when all the words of Jesus, all the signs that he had performed, were condensed into the gesture of breaking the bread and offering the chalice, in anticipation of the sacrifice of the cross, and in these words: "Take, eat; this is my body... Take, drink of it; for this is my blood".

Jesus's gesture at the Last Supper is the ultimate thanksgiving to the Father for his love, for his mercy. "Thanksgiving" in Greek is expressed as "eucharist". And that is why the Sacrament is called the Eucharist: it is the supreme thanksgiving to the Father, who so loved us that he gave us his Son out of love. This is why the term Eucharist includes the whole of that act, which is the act of God and man together, the act of Jesus Christ, true God and true Man.

Memorial and Communion

Therefore the Eucharistic Celebration is much more than simple banquet: it is exactly the memorial of Jesus's Paschal Sacrifice, the mystery at the centre of salvation. "Memorial" does not simply mean a remembrance, a mere memory; it means that every time we celebrate this Sacrament we participate in the mystery of the passion, death and resurrection of Christ. The Eucharist is the summit of God's saving action: the Lord Jesus, by becoming bread broken for us, pours upon us all of his mercy and his love, so as to renew our hearts, our lives and our way of relating with him and with the brethren. It is for this reason that commonly, when we approach this Sacrament, we speak of "receiving Communion", of "taking Communion":

this means that by the power of the Holy Spirit, participation in Holy Communion conforms us in a singular and profound way to Christ, giving us a foretaste already now of the full communion with the Father that characterises the heavenly banquet, where together with all the Saints we will have the joy of contemplating God face-to-face.

Dear friends, we don't ever thank the Lord enough for the gift he has given us in the Eucharist! It is a very great gift and that is why it is so important to go to Mass on Sunday. Go to Mass not just to pray, but to receive Communion, the bread that is the Body of Jesus Christ who saves us, forgives us, unites us to the Father. It is a beautiful thing to do! And we go to Mass every Sunday because that is the day of the resurrection of the Lord. That is why Sunday is so important to us. And in this Eucharist we feel this belonging to the Church, to the People of God, to the Body of God, to Jesus Christ. We will never completely grasp the value and the richness of it. Let us ask him then that this Sacrament continue to keep his presence alive in the Church and to shape our community in charity and communion, according to the Father's heart. This is done throughout life, but is begun on the day of our First Communion. It is important that children be prepared well for their First Communion and that every child receive it, because it is the first step of this intense belonging to Jesus Christ, after Baptism and Confirmation.

How to experience the Eucharist

In the last Catechesis I emphasised how the Eucharist introduces us into real communion with Jesus and his mystery. Now let us ask ourselves several questions that spring from the relationship between the Eucharist that we celebrate and our life, as a Church and as individual Christians. *How do we experience the Eucharist?* When we go to Sunday Mass, how to we live it? Is it only a moment of celebration, an established tradition, an opportunity to find oneself or to feel justified, or is it something more?

Do I love my neighbour?

There are very specific signals for understanding how we are living this, how we experience the Eucharist; signals that tell us if we are living the Eucharist in a good way or not very well. The first indicator is our *way of looking at or considering others*. In the Eucharist, Christ is always renewing his gift of self, which he made on the Cross. His whole life is an act of total sharing of self out of love; thus, he loved to be with his disciples and with the people whom he had a chance to know. This meant for him sharing in their aspirations, their problems, what stirred their soul and their life. Now we, when participating in

Holy Mass, we find ourselves with all sorts of men and women: young people, the elderly, children; poor and well-off; locals and strangers alike; people with their families and people who are alone... But the Eucharist which I celebrate, does it lead me to truly feel they are all like brothers and sisters? Does it increase my capacity to rejoice with those who are rejoicing and cry with those who are crying? Does it urge me to go out to the poor, the sick, the marginalised? Does it help me to recognise in theirs the face of Jesus? We all go to Mass because we love Jesus and we want to share, through the Eucharist, in his passion and his resurrection. But do we love, as Jesus wishes, those brothers and sisters who are the most needy? For example, in Rome these days we have seen much social discomfort either due to the rain, which has caused so much damage to entire districts, or because of the lack of work, a consequence of the global economic crisis. I wonder, and each one of us should wonder: I who go to Mass, how do I live this? Do I try to help, to approach and pray for those in difficulty? Or am I a little indifferent? Or perhaps do I just want to talk: did you see how this or that one is dressed? Sometimes this happens after Mass and it should not! We must concern ourselves with our brothers and sisters who need us because of an illness, a problem. Today, it would do us such good to think of these brothers and sisters of ours who are beset by these problems here in Rome: problems that stem from the grave situation caused by the rain and social instability and unemployment. Let us ask Jesus, whom we receive in the Eucharist, to help us to help them.

Can I forgive and be forgiven?

A second indication, a very important one, is the grace of *feeling forgiven and ready to forgive*. At times someone may ask: "Why must one go to Church, given that those who regularly participate in Holy Mass are still sinners like the others?" We have heard it many times! In reality, the one celebrating the Eucharist doesn't do so because he believes he is or wants to appear better than others, but precisely because he acknowledges that he is always in need of being accepted and reborn by the mercy of God, made flesh in Jesus Christ. If any one of us does not feel in need of the mercy of God, does not see himself as a sinner, it is better for him not to go to Mass! We go to Mass because we are sinners and we want to receive God's pardon, to participate in the redemption of Jesus, in his forgiveness. The "Confession" which we make at the beginning is not "pro forma", it is a real act of repentance! I am a sinner and I confess it, this is how the Mass begins! We should never forget that the Last Supper of Jesus took place "on the night he was betrayed" (1 *Co* 11:23). In the bread and in the wine which we offer and around which we gather, the gift of Christ's body and blood is renewed every time for the remission of our sins. We must go to Mass humbly, like sinners and the Lord reconciles us.

Do I meet Christ?

A last valuable indication comes to us from the relationship between the Eucharistic Celebration and *the life of our Christian communities*. We must always bear in mind that the Eucharist is not something we make; it is not our own commemoration of what Jesus said and did. No. It is precisely an act of Christ! It is Christ who acts there, who is on the altar. It is a gift of Christ, who makes himself present and gathers us around him, to nourish us with his Word and with his life. This means that the mission and the very identity of the Church flows from there, from the Eucharist, and there always takes its shape. A celebration may be flawless on the exterior, very beautiful, but if it does not lead us to encounter Jesus Christ, it is unlikely to bear any kind of nourishment to our heart and our life. Through the Eucharist, however, Christ wishes to enter into our life and permeate it with his grace, so that in every Christian community there may be coherence between liturgy and life.

The heart fills with trust and hope by pondering on Jesus's words recounted in the Gospel: "he who eats my flesh and drinks my blood has eternal life, and I will raise him up at the last day" (*Jn* 6:54). Let us live the Eucharist with the spirit of faith, of prayer, of forgiveness, of repentance, of communal joy, of concern for the needy and for the needs of so many brothers and sisters, in the certainty that the Lord will fulfil what he has promised us: eternal life. So be it!

The Sacrament of Reconciliation

Through the Sacraments of Christian Initiation - Baptism, Confirmation and the Eucharist - man receives new life in Christ. Now, we all know that we carry this life "in earthen vessels" (2 *Co* 4:7), we are still subject to temptation, suffering, and death and, because of sin, we may even lose this new life. That is why the Lord Jesus willed that the Church continue his saving work even to her own members, especially through the Sacrament of Reconciliation and the Anointing of the Sick, which can be united under the heading of "Sacraments of Healing". The Sacrament of Reconciliation is a Sacrament of healing. When I go to confession, it is in order to be healed, to heal my soul, to heal my heart and to be healed of some wrongdoing. The biblical icon which best expresses them in their deep bond is the episode of the forgiving and healing of the paralytic, where the Lord Jesus is revealed at the same time as the physician of souls and of bodies (cf. *Mk* 2:1-12; *Mt* 9:1-8; *Lk* 5:17-26).

Forgiveness is a gift from God

The Sacrament of Penance and Reconciliation flows directly from the Paschal Mystery. In fact, on the evening of Easter the Lord appeared to the disciples, who were locked in the Upper Room, and after addressing them with the greeting, "Peace be with you!", he breathed on them and said: "Receive the Holy Spirit. If you forgive the sins of any, they are forgiven" (*Jn* 20:21-23). This passage reveals to us the most profound dynamic contained in this Sacrament.

First, the fact that the forgiveness of our sins is not something we can give ourselves. I cannot say: I forgive my sins. Forgiveness is asked for, is asked of another, and in Confession we ask for forgiveness from Jesus. Forgiveness is not the fruit of our own efforts but rather a gift, it is a gift of the Holy Spirit who fills us with the wellspring of mercy and of grace that flows unceasingly from the open heart of the Crucified and Risen Christ. Secondly, it reminds us that we can truly be at peace only if we allow ourselves to be reconciled, in the Lord Jesus, with the Father and with the brethren. And we have all felt this in our hearts, when we have gone to confession with a soul weighed down and with a little sadness; and when we receive Jesus's forgiveness we feel at peace, with that peace of soul which is so beautiful, and which only Jesus can give, only Him.

Confession gives peace in Christ

Over time, the celebration of this Sacrament has passed from a public form - because at first it was made publicly

- to a personal one, to the confidential form of Confession. This however does not entail losing the ecclesial matrix that constitutes its vital context. In fact, the Christian community is the place where the Spirit is made present, who renews hearts in the love of God and makes all of the brethren one thing in Christ Jesus. That is why it is not enough to ask the Lord for forgiveness in one's own mind and heart, but why instead it is necessary humbly and trustingly to confess one's sins to a minister of the Church. In the celebration of this Sacrament, the priest represents not only God but also the whole community, who sees itself in the weakness of each of its members, who listens and is moved by his repentance, and who is reconciled with him, which cheers him up and accompanies him on the path of conversion and human and Christian growth. One might say: I confess only to God. Yes, you can say to God "forgive me" and say your sins, but our sins are also committed against the brethren, and against the Church. That is why it is necessary to ask pardon of the Church, and of the brethren in the person of the priest. "But Father, I am ashamed...". Shame is also good, it is healthy to feel a little shame, because being ashamed is salutary. In my country when a person feels no shame, we say that he is 'shameless'; a *'sin verguenza'*. But shame too does good, because it makes us more humble, and the priest receives this confession with love and tenderness and forgives us on God's behalf. Also from a human point of view, in order to unburden oneself, it is good to talk with a brother and tell the priest these things which are weighing so much on my heart. And one feels that one is unburdening oneself before God, with the Church, with his brother. Do not be afraid of Confession! When one is in line to go to Confession, one feels all these things, even shame, but then when one finishes Confession one leaves free, grand, beautiful, forgiven, candid, happy. This is the beauty of Confession! I would like to ask you - but don't say it aloud, everyone respond in his heart: when was the last time you made your confession? Everyone think about it. Two days, two weeks, two years, twenty years, forty years? Everyone count, everyone say: "when was the last time I went to confession?". And if much time has passed, do not lose another day. Go, the priest will be good. Jesus is there, and Jesus is more benevolent than priests, Jesus receives you, he receives you with so much love. Be courageous and go to Confession!

The prodigal son's return

Dear friends, celebrating the Sacrament of Reconciliation means being enfolded in a warm embrace: it is the embrace of the Father's infinite mercy. Let us recall that beautiful, beautiful parable of the son who left his home with the money of his inheritance. He wasted all the money and then, when he had nothing left, he decided to return home, not as a son but as a servant. His heart was filled with so much guilt and shame. The surprise came when he began to speak, to ask for forgiveness, his father did not let him speak, he embraced him, he kissed him, and he began to make merry. But I am telling you: each time we go to confession, God embraces us. God rejoices! Let us go forward on this road. May God bless you!

The Sacrament of the Anointing of the Sick

I would now like to talk to you about the Sacrament of the Anointing of the Sick, which allows us to touch God's compassion for man. In the past it was called "Extreme Unction", because it was understood as a spiritual comfort in the face of imminent death. To speak instead of the "Anointing of the Sick" helps us broaden our vision to include the experience of illness and suffering, within the horizon of God's mercy.

The Good Samaritan

There is a biblical icon that expresses, in all its depths, the mystery that shines through the Anointing of the Sick: it is the parable of the "Good Samaritan" contained in the Gospel of Luke (10:30-35). Each time that we celebrate this Sacrament, the Lord Jesus, in the person of the priest, comes close to the one who suffers and is seriously ill or elderly. The parable says that the Good Samaritan takes care of the suffering man by pouring oil and wine on his wounds. Oil makes us think of that which is blessed by the Bishop each year at the Holy Thursday Chrism Mass, precisely in view of the Anointing of the Sick. Wine, however, is a sign of Christ's love and grace, which flow from the gift of his life for us and are expressed in all their richness in the sacramental life of the Church. Finally, the suffering person is entrusted to an innkeeper, so that he might continue to care for him, sparing no expense. Now, who is this innkeeper? It is the Church, the Christian community - it is us - to whom each day the Lord entrusts those who are afflicted in body and spirit, so that we might lavish all of his mercy and salvation upon them without measure.

The Church is close to the sick

This mandate is repeated in an explicit and precise manner in the Letter of James, where he recommends: "Is any among you sick? Let him call for the elders of the church, and let them pray over him, anointing him with oil in the name of the Lord; and the prayer of faith will save the sick man, and the Lord will raise him up; and if he has committed sins, he will be forgiven" (5:14-15). It was therefore a practice that was already taking place at the time of the Apostles. Jesus in fact taught his disciples to have the same preferential love that he did for the sick and suffering, and he transmitted to them the ability and duty to continue providing, in his name and after his own heart, relief and peace through the special grace of this Sacrament. This, however, should not make us fall into an obsessive search for miracles or the presumption that one can always and in any situation be healed. Rather, it is the reassurance of Jesus's closeness to the sick and the aged, too, because any elderly person, anyone over the age of sixty-five, can receive this Sacrament, through which Jesus himself draws close to us.

Call the priest!

But when someone is sick, we at times think: "Let's call for the priest to come"; "no, then he will bring bad luck, let's not call him", or "he will scare the sick person". Why do we think this? Because the idea is floating about that the undertakers arrive after the priest. And this is not true. The priest comes to help the sick or elderly person; that is why the priest's visit to the sick is so important; we ought to call the priest to the sick person's side and say: "Come, give him the anointing, bless him". It is Jesus himself who comes to relieve the sick person, to give him strength, to give him hope, to help him; and also to forgive his sins. And this is very beautiful! And one must not think that this is taboo, because in times of pain and illness it is always good to know that we are not alone; the priest and those who are present during the Anointing of the Sick, in fact, represent the entire Christian community that as one body huddles around the one who suffers and his family, nurturing their faith and hope, and supporting them through their prayers and fraternal warmth. But the greatest comfort comes from the fact that it is the Lord Jesus himself who makes himself present in the Sacrament, who takes us by the hand, who caresses us as he did with the sick, and who reminds us that we already belong to him and that nothing - not even evil and death - can ever separate us from him. Are we in the habit of calling for the priest so that he might come to our sick - I am not speaking about those who are sick with the flu, for three or four days, but rather about a serious illness - and our elderly, and give them this Sacrament, this comfort, this strength of Jesus to continue on? Let us do so!

Holy Orders

We have already had occasion to point out that the three Sacraments of Baptism, Confirmation and the Eucharist together constitute the mystery of "Christian initiation", a single great event of grace that regenerates us in Christ. This is the fundamental vocation which unites everyone in the Church as disciples of the Lord Jesus. There are then two Sacraments which correspond to two specific vocations: Holy Orders and Matrimony. They constitute two great paths by which the Christian can make his life a gift of love, after the example and in the name of Christ, and thus cooperate in the building up of the Church.

Holy Orders, in its three grades of bishop, priest and deacon, is the Sacrament that enables a man to exercise the ministry which the Lord Jesus entrusted to the Apostles, to shepherd his flock, in the power of his Spirit and according to his Heart. Tending Jesus's flock not by the power of human strength or by one's own power, but by the Spirit's and according to his Heart, the Heart of Jesus which is a heart of love. The priest, the bishop, the deacon must shepherd the Lord's flock with love. It is useless if it is not done with love. And in this sense, the ministers who are chosen and consecrated for this service extend Jesus's presence in time, if they do so by the power of the Holy Spirit, in God's name and with love.

Bishops and priests only lead by serving others

A first aspect. Those who are ordained are placed *at the head of the community*. They are "at the head", yes, but for Jesus this means placing one's authority *at the service* [of the community], as Jesus himself showed and taught his disciples with these words: "You know that the rulers of the Gentiles lord it over them, and their great men exercise authority over them. It shall not be so among you; but whoever would be great among you must be your servant, and whoever would be first among you must be your slave; even as the Son of man came not to be served but to serve, and to give his life as a ransom for many" (*Mt* 20:25-28/*Mk* 10:42-45). A bishop who is not at the service of the community fails to perform his duty; a priest who is not at the service of his community fails to perform his duty, he errs.

Bishops and priests should love the Church as a husband his wife

Another characteristic which also derives from this sacramental union with Christ is a *passionate love for the Church*. Let us think of that passage from the Letter to the Ephesians in which St Paul states that Christ "loved the Church and gave himself up for her, that he might sanctify her, having cleansed her by the washing of water with the word, that he might present the Church to himself in splendour, without spot or wrinkle or any such thing" (5:25-27). Through Holy Orders the minister dedicates himself entirely to his community and loves it with all his heart: it is his family. The bishop and the priest love the Church in their own community, they love it greatly. How? As Christ loves the Church. St Paul will say the same of marriage: the husband is to love his wife as Christ loves the Church. It is a great mystery of love: this of priestly ministry and that of matrimony are two Sacraments, pathways which people normally take to go to the Lord.

Bishops and priests must pray and frequent the sacraments

A final aspect. The Apostle Paul recommends to the disciple Timothy that he not neglect, indeed, that *he always rekindle the gift that is within him*. The gift that he has been given through the laying on of hands (cf. 1 *Tm* 4:14; 2 *Tm* 1:6). When the ministry is not fostered - the ministry of the bishop, the ministry of the priest - through prayer, through listening to the Word of God, through the daily celebration of the Eucharist and also through regularly going to the Sacrament of Penance, he inevitably ends up losing sight of the authentic meaning of his own service and the joy which comes from a profound communion with Jesus.

The bishop who does not pray, the bishop who does not listen to the Word of God, who does not celebrate every day, who does not regularly confess - and the same is true for the priest who does not do these things - in the long run lose their union with Jesus and become so mediocre that they do not benefit the Church. That is why we must help bishops and priests to pray, to listen to the Word of God which is one's daily nourishment, to celebrate the Eucharist each day and to confess regularly. This is so important precisely because it concerns the sanctification of bishops and priests.

A call to service?

I would like to conclude with something which comes to mind: how does one become a priest, where is access to the priesthood sold? No. It is not sold. This is an initiative which the Lord takes. The Lord calls. He calls each of those whom he wills to become priests. Perhaps there are some young men present here who have heard this call in their hearts, the aspiration to become a priest, the desire to serve others in the things of God, the desire to spend one's entire life in service in order to catechise, baptise, forgive, celebrate the Eucharist, heal the sick ...the whole of one's life in this way. If some of you have heard this call in your heart, it is Jesus who has placed it there. Pay attention to this invitation and pray that it might grow and bear fruit for the whole Church.

Matrimony

We conclude the series of catecheses on the Sacraments by speaking about Matrimony. This Sacrament leads us to the heart of God's design, which is a plan for a Covenant with his people, with us all, a plan for communion. At the beginning of the Book of Genesis, the first book of the Bible, at the culmination of the creation account it says: "God created man in his own image, in the image of God he created him; male and female he created them...Therefore a man leaves his father and his mother and cleaves to his wife, and they become one flesh" (*Gn* 1:27; 2:24). The image of God is the married couple: the man and the woman; not only the man, not only the woman, but both of them together. This is the image of God: love, God's covenant with us is represented in that covenant between man and woman. And this is very beautiful! We are created in order to love, as a reflection of God and his love. And in the marital union man and woman fulfil this vocation through their mutual reciprocity and their full and definitive communion of life.

A married couple is an image of God

When a man and woman celebrate the Sacrament of Matrimony, God is as it were "mirrored" in them; he impresses in them his own features and the indelible character of his love. Marriage is the icon of God's love for us. Indeed, God is communion too: the three Persons of the Father, the Son and the Holy Spirit live eternally in perfect unity. And this is precisely the mystery of Matrimony: God makes of the two spouses one single life. The Bible uses a powerful expression and says "one flesh", so intimate is the union between man and woman in marriage. And this is precisely the mystery of marriage: the love of God which is reflected in the couple that decides to live together. Therefore a man leaves his home, the home of his parents, and goes to live with his wife and unites himself so strongly to her that the two become - the Bible says - one flesh.

A married couple is an image of the Church

St Paul, in the Letter to the Ephesians, emphasises that a great mystery is reflected in Christian spouses: the relationship established by Christ with the Church, a nuptial relationship (cf. *Ep* 5:21-33). The Church is the bride of Christ. This is their relationship. This means that Matrimony responds to a specific vocation and must be considered as a consecration (cf. *Gaudium et Spes*, n. 48: *Familiaris Consortio*, n. 56). It is a consecration: the man and woman are consecrated in their love. The spouses, in fact, in virtue of the Sacrament, are invested with a true and proper mission, so that starting with the simple ordinary things of life they may make visible the love with which Christ loves His Church, by continuing to give his life for her in fidelity and service.

Prayer, making peace, and the three magic words

There is a truly marvellous design inherent in the Sacrament of Matrimony! And it unfolds in the simplicity and frailty of the human condition. We are well aware of how many difficulties two spouses experience. The important thing is to keep alive their bond with God, who stands as the foundation of the marital bond. And the true bond is always the Lord. When the family prays, the bond is preserved. When the husband prays for his wife and the wife prays for her husband, that bond becomes strong; one praying for the other. It is true that there are so many difficulties in married life, so many, when there is insufficient work or money, when the children have problems. So much to contend with. And many times the husband and wife become a little fractious and argue between themselves. They argue, this is how it is, there is always arguing in marriage, sometimes the plates even fly. Yet we must not become saddened by this, this is the human condition. The secret is that love is stronger than the moment when there is arguing, and therefore I always advise spouses: do not let a day when you have argued end without making peace. Always! And to make peace it isn't necessary to call the United Nations to come to the house and make peace.

A little gesture is sufficient, a caress, and then let it be! Until tomorrow! And tomorrow begin again. And this is life, carrying on, carrying on with courage and the desire to live together. And this is truly great, it is beautiful! Married life is such a beautiful thing and we must treasure it always, treasure the children. On other occasions in this Square I have mentioned something else which is so helpful for marriage. There are three words that always need to be said, three words that need to be said at home: may I, thank you, and sorry. The three magic words. *May I*: so as not to be intrusive in the life of the spouses. May I, but how does it seem to you? May I, please allow me. *Thank you*: to thank one's spouse; thank you for what you did for me, thank you for this. That beauty of giving thanks! And since we all make mistakes, that other word which is a bit hard to say but which needs to be said: *sorry*. Please, thank you, and sorry. With these three words, with the prayer of the husband for the wife and vice versa, by always making peace before the day comes to an end, marriage will go forward. The three magic words, prayer and always making peace. May the Lord bless you, and pray for me.

Catechesis on the Sacraments:

Saint Peter's Square, Wednesday, 8th January 2014
Saint Peter's Square, Wednesday, 15th January 2014
Saint Peter's Square, Wednesday, 29th January 2014
Saint Peter's Square, Wednesday, 5th February 2014
Saint Peter's Square, Wednesday, 12th February 2014
Saint Peter's Square, Wednesday, 19th February 2014
Saint Peter's Square, Wednesday, 26th February 2014
Saint Peter's Square, Wednesday, 26th March 2014
Saint Peter's Square, Wednesday, 2nd April 2014